Fundamentals And Methods Of Self-Defense: From Basics To Advanced Techniques

QIÁNG ZǏMÒ

Copyright © 2024 By Qiáng Zǐmò

All Rights Reserved

Table of Contents

Introductory 5
CHAPTER ONE 8
  Philosophical Underpinnings 8
  Core Principles Of Jow-Ga 12
CHAPTER TWO 17
  Spiritual And Mental Aspects 17
  Stances And Footwork 22
CHAPTER THREE 28
  Hand & Leg Techniques 28
  Basic Forms (Katas) 35
CHAPTER FOUR 40
  Combination Techniques 40
  Defensive & Offensive Strategies 45
CHAPTER FIVE 53
  Power Generation And Internal Energy (Qi) 53
  Iron Body And Conditioning 60
CHAPTER SIX 66
  Application Of Techniques In Sparring 66
  Weapons Training, Techniques And Forms With Weapons 71

CHAPTER SEVEN **79**

Practical Application And Strategy With Weapons 79

Integration Of Jow-Ga Into Everyday Life .. 86

Summary 93

THE END **96**

Introductory

Jow-Ga Kung Fu, alternatively referred to as Chow Gar Kung Fu, is an ancient martial art with roots in Southern China. It is distinguished by its emphasis on close-range combat, low stances, and swift and forceful attacks.

The aesthetic is a synthesis of two significant influences:

• Jow Family Style: Established by Jow Lung during the late Qing Dynasty (circa the late 1800s), this style places significant emphasis on robust and forceful methodologies. It employs direct and unambiguous techniques, including strikes, kicks, and blocks.

• Hung Ga Style: Alternatively referred to as Hung Gar, this style derives its nomenclature from its progenitor, the Shaolin Kung Fu master Hung Hei-Gun. Hung Ga is renowned for its incorporation of animal-inspired movements, forceful hand strikes, and strong stances.

Jow-Ga Kung Fu integrates components from both of these styles, including dynamic footwork, forceful stances, and strong hand techniques. It emphasizes conditioning, practical applications of self-defense, and the philosophy of traditional Chinese martial arts.

Typical Jow-Ga Kung Fu training consists of conditioning exercises, partner routines, sparring, and the rehearsal of form sequences. Similar to other conventional martial arts, this style places equal emphasis on character development, discipline, and respect in addition to physical training.

CHAPTER ONE
Philosophical Underpinnings

Jow-Ga Kung Fu is grounded in traditional Chinese martial arts principles, which originate from the philosophical underpinnings of Daoism and Confucianism. Key elements comprising the philosophical underpinnings of Jow-Ga Kung Fu are as follows:

• Taoism, or Daoism: Daoism places significant emphasis on the notion of Dao, an appellation that translates to "the Way." This principle manifests itself frequently in martial arts through the concepts of embracing the natural progression of events, adjusting to fluctuations, and preserving equilibrium. To achieve optimal effectiveness, practitioners of Jow-Ga Kung Fu may strive to harmonize their movements with the natural flow of energy while exerting minimal effort.

- Incorporation of Confucian values, including humility, respect, and integrity, is a prevalent aspect of Jow-Ga Kung Fu training. Students are motivated to develop virtuous qualities of character and to demonstrate respect and dignity towards others. Personal development and martial arts practice are both dependent on the self-discipline, perseverance, and commitment to continuous learning that are emphasized in Confucian principles.

- Buddhist Influence: Although Jow-Ga Kung Fu does not overtly label itself as Buddhist, certain tenets of Buddhist philosophy, including compassion and mindfulness, might exert an impact on the training regimen. Through practice, practitioners may hope to attain mental clarity, concentration, and an inner calm. Additionally, their approach to self-defense and conflict resolution may be influenced by the ethical principles of nonviolence and compassion towards all beings.

- Yin-Yang Philosophy: Chinese martial arts are founded upon the concept of Yin and Yang, which symbolize the equilibrium between complementary polarities. The objective of Jow-Ga

Kung Fu is to strike a balance between gentle and hard techniques, speed and strength, and offense and defense. In addition to physical techniques, this equilibrium is also evident in the mental and spiritual dimensions of training.

Overall, the philosophical underpinnings of Jow-Ga Kung Fu emphasize the cultivation of moral character, mental discipline, and spiritual awareness in addition to physical prowess and martial expertise. Off the training field, these principles direct practitioners in their pursuit of self-improvement and holistic growth.

Core Principles Of Jow-Ga

The core principles of Jow-Ga Kung Fu revolve around practicality, efficiency, and balance in combat, as well as the cultivation of character and discipline in practitioners. Here are some of the key principles:

• **Directness and Simplicity**: Jow-Ga Kung Fu emphasizes direct and efficient techniques that are easy to learn and apply effectively in real combat situations. Movements are kept simple and streamlined to minimize unnecessary flourishes and maximize practicality.

• **Power and Speed**: Techniques in Jow-Ga Kung Fu are executed with a combination of speed and power.

Strikes are delivered explosively, generating maximum force in minimal time. This emphasis on power and speed enhances the effectiveness of offensive and defensive techniques.

- **Stability and Balance**: Jow-Ga Kung Fu emphasizes strong stances and balance, which are essential for generating power, maintaining control, and withstanding attacks. Practitioners are taught to root themselves firmly to the ground while remaining agile and mobile.

- **Combination of Hard and Soft**: Jow-Ga Kung Fu incorporates both hard (external) and soft (internal) techniques. Hard techniques involve powerful strikes and blocks, while soft techniques focus on redirecting an opponent's force and using their momentum against them. The integration of these elements creates a versatile and adaptable fighting style.

- **Close-Range Combat**: Jow-Ga Kung Fu specializes in close-range combat, where strikes, locks, and throws are executed at close quarters. Practitioners are trained to engage opponents in tight spaces and to control the distance to their advantage.

- **Conditioning and Fitness**: Physical conditioning is an integral part of Jow-Ga Kung Fu training. Practitioners undergo rigorous workouts to build strength, endurance, flexibility, and agility. A strong and healthy body is seen as essential for martial proficiency and overall well-being.

- **Character Development**: Beyond physical techniques, Jow-Ga Kung Fu places a strong emphasis on the development of character and morality. Practitioners are expected to cultivate virtues such as respect, humility, discipline, and perseverance both inside and outside the training hall.

- **Continuous Learning and Improvement**: Jow-Ga Kung Fu is regarded as a lifelong journey of self-discovery and improvement. Practitioners are encouraged to remain open-minded, to learn from their experiences, and to constantly refine their skills and understanding of the art.

On the basis of these Jow-Ga Kung Fu fundamental principles, practitioners construct their abilities, character, and mentality, thereby attaining the status of virtuous individuals and proficient martial artists.

CHAPTER TWO
Spiritual And Mental Aspects

Jow-Ga Kung Fu spots equal importance on mental and spiritual dimensions as essential constituents of training, alongside physical techniques and philosophical principles. The following are several pivotal components:

• Concentration and Focus: Jow-Ga Kung Fu practice demands an exceptional degree of concentration and focus. By developing the ability to calm the mind and concentrate intently on their movements, students improve their combat awareness and responsiveness. Furthermore, this cognitive discipline extends to various spheres of life, enhancing focus and efficiency.

- Mindfulness and Presence: Practises of Jow-Ga Kung Fu are advised to develop an awareness of the present moment and mindfulness. Through maintaining complete mindfulness in the present moment, pupils are able to respond more efficiently to evolving circumstances and execute judicious decisions in combat. Additionally to reducing stress and fostering inner calm, mindfulness practice is beneficial to mental and emotional health.

- The application of visualization techniques and mental imagery is a prevalent practice in Jow-Ga Kung Fu, serving to augment skill development and performance. Through the process of visualizing themselves performing techniques with accuracy and efficacy, students strengthen neural connections and enhance their muscle memory. Practicing this idea in one's mind not only improves physical execution but also instills a sense of assurance and conviction.

- Energy Management and Breath Control: In Jow-Ga Kung Fu, the implementation of correct breathing techniques is critical for the purposes of energy regulation, relaxation promotion, and power maximization. Students are instructed in the art of coordinating their breath with their movements, employing deep diaphragmatic breathing as a means to enhance oxygen delivery to the musculature and sustain endurance throughout combat and training. Additionally, breath control promotes mental tranquility and an inner sense of equilibrium.

• Spiritual Development and Introspection: Jow-Ga Kung Fu affords individuals the chance to engage in spiritual development and introspection. By engaging in consistent exercise and self-reflection, learners acquire a deeper understanding of their merits, deficiencies, and opportunities for growth. Engaging in martial arts training facilitates a process of introspection and individual growth, culminating in an enhanced sense of self-knowledge and control.

• Delight in Traditional Lineage and Culture: A significant number of Jow-Ga Kung Fu practitioners place great importance on their affiliation with the art's illustrious cultural heritage and lineage. Through the study of traditional forms, techniques, and philosophy, students gain a more profound understanding of the history and culture of Chinese martial arts. An enhanced sense of affiliation and personal identity is fostered by this connection within the martial arts community.

In general, the incorporation of mental and spiritual dimensions into Jow-Ga Kung Fu serves to enhance the physical training, aiding in the holistic development of individuals who acquire not only martial arts prowess but also equilibrium and inner peace. Through the harmonious development of the mind, body, and spirit, martial arts students have the potential to attain comprehensive growth and a sense of fulfillment.

Stances And Footwork

Stances and footwork are fundamental components of Jow-Ga Kung Fu, playing a crucial role in generating power, maintaining balance, and executing techniques effectively. Here are some common stances and footwork principles found in Jow-Ga Kung Fu:

• **Horse Stance (Ma Bu)**: The horse stance is a foundational stance in Jow-Ga Kung Fu, characterized by a wide and low stance with the feet planted firmly on the ground. The knees are bent, and the back is straight, creating a stable base for generating power in strikes and maintaining balance during movement. Practitioners often hold the horse stance for extended periods to develop leg strength, endurance, and stability.

• **Bow Stance (Gong Bu)**: The bow stance is another essential stance used in Jow-Ga Kung Fu, often employed when executing forward or diagonal strikes. In this stance, one leg is extended forward with the knee bent, while the other leg is positioned behind with the knee slightly bent. The weight is distributed evenly between both legs, allowing for mobility, power generation, and balance.

- **Cat Stance (Xie Bu)**: The cat stance is a transitional stance used for quick changes in direction or to evade attacks. In this stance, the weight is primarily on one leg, with the other leg raised slightly and the toes touching the ground for balance. The body is kept low, with the knees bent, facilitating rapid movement and agility.

- **Tiger Stance (Hu Bu)**: The tiger stance is a low and wide stance used for stability and power in close-range combat. In this stance, the feet are positioned wider than shoulder-width apart, with the knees deeply bent and the torso leaning slightly forward. The stance provides a strong foundation for delivering powerful strikes and grappling techniques.

- **Footwork Principles**: Footwork in Jow-Ga Kung Fu emphasizes agility, speed, and precision in movement. Practitioners are trained to step with purpose, maintaining balance and stability while transitioning between stances and executing techniques. Footwork drills often involve practicing forward, backward, lateral, and circular movements to develop coordination and fluidity in motion.

• **Pivoting and Turning**: Jow-Ga Kung Fu incorporates pivoting and turning movements to angle off from attacks, evade opponents, or reposition for better leverage. Practitioners learn to pivot on the balls of their feet, maintaining balance and control while changing direction quickly. Pivoting allows practitioners to maintain their centerline and adjust their position relative to the opponent's movements.

• **Dynamic Movement**: Jow-Ga Kung Fu encourages dynamic and explosive footwork, enabling practitioners to close the distance, create openings, and generate power in their attacks. By combining swift footwork with proper body mechanics, practitioners can move fluidly and efficiently in combat, maintaining a tactical advantage over their opponents.

Overall, stances and footwork are essential elements of Jow-Ga Kung Fu, providing practitioners with a solid foundation for executing techniques, maintaining balance and stability, and navigating effectively in combat situations. Through dedicated practice and refinement, students develop agility, speed, and precision in their movement, enhancing their overall martial arts proficiency.

CHAPTER THREE
Hand & Leg Techniques

In Jow-Ga Kung Fu, both hand and leg techniques are integral parts of the martial art's arsenal, designed to deliver powerful strikes, blocks, and counters. Here are some common hand and leg techniques used in Jow-Ga Kung Fu:

Hand Techniques:

- **Straight Punch (Chun Choy)**: The straight punch is a fundamental hand technique in Jow-Ga Kung Fu, executed with a straight and direct motion. Practitioners deliver punches using the knuckles of the fist, aiming for vital targets such as the nose, chin, or solar plexus.

- **Hook Punch (Gwor Choy)**: The hook punch is a circular striking technique used to target an opponent's head or body from a lateral angle. Practitioners generate power by rotating the body and arm, delivering the punch in a looping motion.

- **Upper Cut (Tong Choy)**: The uppercut is a short-range punching technique used to strike upward toward an opponent's chin or body. Practitioners drive the fist upward from a lower position, aiming to deliver a powerful blow to the target area.

- **Backfist Strike (Tai Choy)**: The backfist strike involves striking with the back of the closed fist, usually delivered with a whipping motion. This technique is effective for targeting the temple, jaw, or nose of an opponent, often used in close-range combat situations.

- **Palm Strike (Zhang Choy)**: The palm strike is a hand technique where the palm of the hand is used to strike the opponent's face, chest, or abdomen. This technique can be executed with a thrusting motion or a slapping motion, depending on the situation.

- **Knifehand Strike (Dang Choy)**: The knifehand strike involves striking with the edge of the hand, resembling the edge of a knife. Practitioners can deliver knifehand strikes to various targets, such as the neck, collarbone, or temple, with both the lead and rear hand.

Leg Techniques:

• **Front Kick (Ting Juk)**: The front kick is a basic kicking technique in Jow-Ga Kung Fu, delivered with the ball of the foot or the instep. Practitioners thrust the leg forward to strike the opponent's midsection, groin, or knee with speed and power.

• **Side Kick (Peng Juk)**: The side kick is a lateral kicking technique used to strike the opponent's body from the side. Practitioners lift the knee to the side and extend the leg outward, aiming to hit the target with the heel or the edge of the foot.

- **Roundhouse Kick (Wan Juk)**: The roundhouse kick is a versatile kicking technique that involves a circular motion of the leg, striking the opponent's body with the shin or the top of the foot. Practitioners can target various areas, including the ribs, thighs, or head, depending on the trajectory of the kick.

- **Back Kick (Hou Juk)**: The back kick is a powerful kicking technique executed by thrusting the leg backward toward the opponent. Practitioners pivot on the supporting foot and drive the heel or the bottom of the foot into the target, delivering a forceful blow.

- **Sweeping Kick (Tai Juk)**: The sweeping kick is a technique used to sweep the opponent's legs out from under them, causing them to lose balance and fall to the ground. Practitioners use the lower part of the leg to sweep across the opponent's ankles or shins, disrupting their stance and control.

• **Flying Kick (Fei Juk)**: The flying kick is an advanced kicking technique that involves leaping into the air and delivering a powerful kick to the opponent. Practitioners use momentum and timing to execute flying kicks with precision and force, often targeting the head or upper body.

These hand and leg techniques in Jow-Ga Kung Fu are honed through dedicated practice, focusing on speed, power, accuracy, and timing. By mastering these techniques, practitioners develop a formidable repertoire of offensive and defensive skills for self-defense and combat.

Basic Forms (Katas)

In Jow-Ga Kung Fu, practitioners learn a variety of forms, also known as katas, which are choreographed sequences of movements that simulate combat scenarios.

These forms serve multiple purposes, including developing muscle memory, refining technique, and transmitting martial knowledge from one generation to the next. Here are some basic forms commonly practiced in Jow-Ga Kung Fu:

- **Siu Fook Fu**: Also known as "Little Tiger Taming the Wind," Siu Fook Fu is one of the foundational forms in Jow-Ga Kung Fu. It focuses on fundamental stances, blocks, strikes, and footwork, teaching basic techniques and principles to beginners.

- **Nga Jung Set**: This form, known as the "Five Animals Set," incorporates movements inspired by the characteristics of five animals: tiger, crane, leopard, snake, and dragon. Each animal represents different techniques and attributes, such as power, agility, and flexibility. The Nga Jung Set emphasizes versatility and adaptability in combat.

- **Gung Ji Fook Fu**: Translating to "Taming the Wind Under the Arm," Gung Ji Fook Fu is a dynamic form that emphasizes close-range combat techniques, including grappling, joint locks, and throws. It teaches practitioners how to control and neutralize opponents at close quarters.

• **Fu Hok Seung Ying Kuen**: Known as the "Tiger and Crane Double Form," Fu Hok Seung Ying Kuen combines the power of the tiger with the grace of the crane. This form integrates strong, aggressive movements with fluid, evasive techniques, representing the harmonious balance between hard and soft styles.

• **Ng Long Ba Gwa Cheung**: This form, named the "Five Dragons Baguazhang," incorporates circular footwork patterns and evasive movements inspired by Baguazhang, a Chinese internal martial art. It emphasizes circularity, continuous motion, and strategic positioning to outmaneuver opponents.

• **Luk Hap Ba Fa Kuen**: Translating to "Six Harmony Eight Methods Fist," Luk Hap Ba Fa Kuen is a comprehensive form that integrates techniques from various martial arts styles, including Jow-Ga Kung Fu, Tai Chi, and Wing Chun. It emphasizes adaptability and versatility, teaching practitioners how to respond effectively to different combat situations.

• **Tiet Sin Kuen**: Also known as "Iron Wire Fist," Tiet Sin Kuen is an advanced form that focuses on internal energy cultivation and striking techniques. It emphasizes breathing, visualization, and mental focus to develop internal power and resilience.

These forms represent just a sample of the diverse repertoire of forms practiced in Jow-Ga Kung Fu. Each form is designed to teach specific techniques, principles, and concepts, helping practitioners develop a well-rounded skill set for self-defense and martial arts practice. As students progress in their training, they learn additional forms that build upon the foundational movements and deepen their understanding of the art.

CHAPTER FOUR
Combination Techniques

Combination techniques in Jow-Ga Kung Fu involve the seamless integration of various strikes, blocks, kicks, and footwork patterns to create effective offensive and defensive sequences. These combinations are designed to flow smoothly from one technique to the next, allowing practitioners to maintain pressure on their opponents while exploiting openings and creating opportunities for counterattacks. Here are some common combination techniques used in Jow-Ga Kung Fu:

• **Jab-Cross-Hook Combination**: This classic combination involves a straight punch (jab), followed by a straight punch with the rear hand (cross), and finished with a hook punch. Practitioners use the jab to set up the cross, which sets up the hook to target the opponent's head or body from different angles.

• **Low Kick-High Kick Combination**: This combination starts with a low kick targeting the opponent's legs or body, followed by a high kick aimed at the head or upper body. By varying the target and trajectory of the kicks, practitioners can keep their opponents off-balance and create openings for further attacks.

• **Block-Counter Combination**: When faced with an opponent's attack, practitioners can use a blocking technique to deflect the incoming strike, immediately followed by a counterattack. For example, after blocking a punch with a forearm block, practitioners can counter with a straight punch or a kick to exploit the opponent's exposed areas.

• **Feint-Strike Combination**: Feinting involves faking an attack or movement to deceive the opponent and create openings for subsequent strikes. Practitioners can use feints to set up combinations, such as feinting a low kick to draw the opponent's guard down before delivering a high kick or punch.

- **Combination Strikes with Footwork**: Effective combination techniques often incorporate footwork to maintain optimal positioning and angles of attack. Practitioners may use stepping or pivoting movements to evade an opponent's strikes while simultaneously launching their own counterattacks, creating opportunities for follow-up techniques.

- **Chain Punching Combination**: Chain punching involves delivering a rapid series of punches in quick succession, typically targeting the opponent's centerline. Practitioners maintain forward pressure and momentum while continuously striking with alternating hands, overwhelming the opponent's defenses and keeping them off-balance.

- **Counter-Attack Combination**: In Jow-Ga Kung Fu, counter-attacking is a key principle, and combination techniques often involve countering an opponent's attack with simultaneous or consecutive strikes. Practitioners capitalize on openings created by the opponent's movements to launch their own offensive combinations, exploiting vulnerabilities and maintaining control of the engagement.

These combination techniques in Jow-Ga Kung Fu are practiced through repetition, drilling, and sparring, allowing practitioners to develop fluidity, timing, and adaptability in applying techniques in dynamic combat situations. By mastering these combinations, practitioners can effectively engage opponents, control the pace of the fight, and maximize their chances of success in self-defense or competition.

Defensive & Offensive Strategies

In Jow-Ga Kung Fu, practitioners employ a variety of defensive and offensive strategies to effectively engage opponents, control the pace of the fight, and maximize their chances of success in combat.

These strategies encompass a range of techniques, tactics, and principles aimed at both protecting oneself from harm and delivering effective attacks.

Here are some common defensive and offensive strategies used in Jow-Ga Kung Fu:

Defensive Strategies:

• **Blocking and Parrying**: Blocking involves using arms, hands, or legs to intercept and deflect incoming strikes from opponents. Practitioners utilize various blocking techniques such as forearm blocks, palm blocks, and leg blocks to minimize the impact of attacks and create openings for counterattacks. Parrying involves redirecting an opponent's strike away from its intended target using controlled deflections and angles.

- **Evading and Dodging**: Evading techniques involve moving the body out of the path of an opponent's attack, typically through stepping, leaning, or shifting weight. Practitioners employ evasive footwork and head movement to avoid incoming strikes while maintaining optimal positioning for counterattacks. Dodging techniques involve quick, fluid movements to slip past attacks and create angles for retaliation.

- **Clinching and Grappling**: In close-range combat situations, practitioners may use clinching and grappling techniques to control opponents and neutralize their attacks.

Clinching involves securing a tight grip on the opponent's body, limiting their mobility and opportunities for striking. Grappling techniques such as joint locks, throws, and sweeps are employed to off-balance opponents and gain dominant positions.

- **Intercepting and Disrupting**: Intercepting techniques involve preemptively striking or disrupting an opponent's movement before they can execute their intended attack. Practitioners use quick, decisive actions to intercept opponents' movements, disrupting their timing and rhythm. Techniques such as jamming punches, checking kicks, and intercepting footwork are commonly employed to thwart opponents' advances.

Offensive Strategies:

• **Combination Attacks**: Offensive strategies in Jow-Ga Kung Fu often revolve around delivering fluid, dynamic combinations of strikes, kicks, and grappling techniques to overwhelm opponents and create openings for further attacks. Practitioners chain together various techniques, seamlessly transitioning between offensive and defensive actions to maintain pressure and control.

• **Targeting Vulnerabilities**: Effective offensive strategies involve identifying and exploiting opponents' weaknesses and vulnerabilities. Practitioners aim for key targets such as the head, ribs, solar plexus, and joints to maximize the impact of their attacks and incapacitate opponents. By targeting vulnerable areas, practitioners can disrupt opponents' balance, impair their mobility, and weaken their defenses.

- **Feints and Deception**: Offensive strategies may incorporate feints and deception to bait opponents into committing to defensive movements or exposing openings. Practitioners use feints to create illusions of attack, drawing out reactions from opponents and capitalizing on their responses to launch effective counterattacks.

- **Pressure and Control**: Maintaining forward pressure and controlling the pace of the fight are essential offensive strategies in Jow-Ga Kung Fu. Practitioners apply relentless pressure on opponents, dictating the flow of the engagement and forcing them into defensive positions. By controlling the distance, timing, and angles of engagement, practitioners can effectively set up and execute their offensive techniques.

- **Adaptation and Flexibility**: Effective offensive strategies require adaptability and flexibility to respond to changing circumstances and opponents' actions. Practitioners adjust their tactics and techniques based on opponents' strengths, weaknesses, and tendencies, exploiting opportunities and adjusting their approach as needed to achieve success in combat.

By combining defensive and offensive strategies in Jow-Ga Kung Fu, practitioners can effectively navigate combat situations, protect themselves from harm, and exert control over opponents, ultimately enhancing their overall martial prowess and ability to defend themselves in real-world scenarios.

CHAPTER FIVE
Power Generation And Internal Energy (Qi)

In Jow-Ga Kung Fu, power generation is a critical aspect of martial proficiency, and practitioners utilize various physical and internal methods to generate force in their techniques. Additionally, while Jow-Ga Kung Fu is primarily an external martial art, some practitioners also explore concepts of internal energy, often referred to as "Qi" (or "Chi"). Here's an overview of power generation and internal energy in Jow-Ga Kung Fu:

Power Generation:

- **Body Mechanics**: Power generation in Jow-Ga Kung Fu begins with proper body mechanics. Practitioners learn to coordinate their movements efficiently, utilizing the entire body to generate force rather than relying solely on isolated muscle strength. Techniques such as rotating the hips, transferring weight, and coordinating breath with movement maximize the effectiveness of strikes, blocks, and other techniques.

- **Rooting**: Rooting is the ability to establish a stable connection with the ground, providing a solid foundation for generating power. Practitioners learn to sink their weight and maintain a low center of gravity, allowing them to root themselves firmly to the ground and channel force effectively through their stances and techniques.

- **Structure and Alignment**: Proper alignment of the body is essential for optimizing power generation. Practitioners maintain correct posture and alignment, ensuring that energy flows smoothly through the kinetic chain without encountering resistance or inefficiencies. Techniques are executed with precision and economy of motion to maximize power and minimize wasted effort.

- **Speed and Timing**: Power in Jow-Ga Kung Fu is not only about raw strength but also about speed and timing. Practitioners develop explosive speed in their techniques, accelerating rapidly from relaxed positions to generate maximum force upon impact. Timing is crucial for synchronizing movements with opponents' actions, exploiting openings, and maximizing the effectiveness of techniques.

- **Conditioning**: Physical conditioning plays a vital role in power generation. Practitioners undergo rigorous strength training, flexibility training, and conditioning exercises to develop the strength, endurance, and agility necessary for martial proficiency. Strong muscles, flexible joints, and resilient tendons and ligaments contribute to the ability to generate power efficiently and effectively.

Internal Energy (Qi):

While Jow-Ga Kung Fu is primarily an external martial art focused on physical techniques, some practitioners also explore concepts of internal energy, commonly referred to as "Qi" or "Chi." Internal training in Jow-Ga Kung Fu involves cultivating awareness of breath, relaxation, and mental focus to enhance physical performance and overall well-being. Here are some ways in which internal energy concepts may be integrated into Jow-Ga Kung Fu practice:

• **Breath Control**: Practitioners learn to regulate their breathing to synchronize with movement, promote relaxation, and facilitate energy flow.

Deep diaphragmatic breathing is emphasized to oxygenate the muscles, calm the mind, and enhance overall vitality.

- **Mindfulness and Concentration**: Internal training in Jow-Ga Kung Fu involves cultivating mindfulness and mental focus to enhance awareness, sensitivity, and responsiveness in combat. Practitioners develop the ability to maintain a calm, centered state of mind amidst the chaos of combat, allowing for more effective execution of techniques and strategies.

- **Visualization and Mental Imagery**: Visualization techniques are used to enhance power generation and technique execution. Practitioners visualize energy flowing through the body, envisioning successful execution of techniques with clarity and precision. Mental imagery reinforces neural pathways and enhances muscle memory, improving overall performance.

• **Energy Circulation**: Internal training may involve practices to cultivate and circulate Qi throughout the body's energy channels (meridians). Techniques such as Qigong (energy cultivation exercises), Neigong (internal strength training), and Tai Chi (slow, meditative movement) are sometimes incorporated into Jow-Ga Kung Fu training to promote health, vitality, and martial prowess.

It's important to note that the exploration of internal energy concepts in Jow-Ga Kung Fu varies among practitioners and instructors, and not all practitioners may focus on or prioritize these aspects in their training. However, for those who do incorporate internal training, it can provide additional insights, depth, and benefits to their martial arts practice.

Iron Body And Conditioning

Iron body training, also known as "Iron Shirt" or "Iron Body Conditioning," is a method used in some traditional Chinese martial arts, including Jow-Ga Kung Fu, to strengthen the body's resilience and ability to withstand physical impact. The goal of iron body training is to develop dense muscles, toughen the skin, and condition the bones, tendons, and internal organs to reduce susceptibility to injury from strikes, blows, and other forms of physical trauma. Here's an overview of iron body training and conditioning methods in Jow-Ga Kung Fu:

- **Iron Palm**: Iron palm training focuses on toughening the hands and forearms to withstand impact and deliver powerful strikes. Practitioners perform repetitive striking exercises on various surfaces, such as sandbags, gravel, or special conditioning bags filled with materials like beans, iron shot, or lead pellets. Over time, this practice increases bone density, toughens the skin, and strengthens the muscles and connective tissues of the hands and forearms.

- **Iron Body Conditioning**: Iron body training involves striking or receiving blows to different parts of the body to desensitize nerves, strengthen muscles, and condition the bones and connective tissues. Practitioners may use methods such as striking their own body with fists, elbows, knees, or other body parts, or having a training partner deliver controlled strikes to specific areas of the body. Gradual progression and proper technique are essential to avoid injury and achieve desired results.

- **Breathing and Meditation**: Breathing techniques and meditation are integral components of iron body training in Jow-Ga Kung Fu. Practitioners learn to regulate their breath to promote relaxation, focus, and energy circulation throughout the body. Meditation practices help cultivate mental resilience, concentration, and inner strength, enhancing the effectiveness of iron body training and overall martial arts practice.

- **Herbal Liniments and Salves**: Herbal liniments and salves are often used to facilitate recovery and enhance the effects of iron body training. These topical preparations contain a combination of herbs and medicinal ingredients known for their anti-inflammatory, analgesic, and tissue-healing properties. They are applied to the skin before and after training to reduce bruising, inflammation, and soreness, and promote faster recovery.

- **Gradual Progression**: Iron body training in Jow-Ga Kung Fu follows a principle of gradual progression, starting with lighter intensity and gradually increasing intensity and duration over time. Practitioners begin with basic conditioning exercises and gradually advance to more challenging techniques as their bodies adapt and become more resilient. Consistent, disciplined practice is essential to achieve significant results in iron body conditioning.

It's important to note that iron body training should be approached with caution and under the guidance of a qualified instructor to ensure safety and effectiveness. Improper training techniques or excessive force can lead to serious injury or long-term damage. Additionally, while iron body training can improve physical resilience and martial effectiveness, it is not a substitute for proper technique, strategy, and overall martial arts skill development in Jow-Ga Kung Fu.

CHAPTER SIX
Application Of Techniques In Sparring

In Jow-Ga Kung Fu, the application of techniques in sparring, also known as "san shou" or "free sparring," is an essential component of martial arts training. Sparring allows practitioners to test and refine their skills in a controlled, dynamic environment against resisting opponents. Here's how techniques are applied in sparring in Jow-Ga Kung Fu:

• **Adaptation to Rules and Safety**: Sparring sessions in Jow-Ga Kung Fu typically have specific rules and safety guidelines to ensure the well-being of participants. These rules may vary depending on the level of experience, the intensity of the sparring session, and the goals of training. Practitioners learn to adapt their techniques and strategies to comply with sparring rules while effectively engaging opponents.

• **Dynamic Application of Techniques**: Sparring in Jow-Ga Kung Fu involves the dynamic application of various techniques learned in training, including strikes, kicks, blocks, footwork, and defensive maneuvers. Practitioners employ a combination of offensive and defensive tactics to control the distance, set up attacks, and counter opponents' movements.

• **Combination and Flow**: Effective sparring in Jow-Ga Kung Fu often involves chaining together combinations of techniques to create openings and overwhelm opponents. Practitioners seamlessly transition between strikes, kicks, and blocks, maintaining fluidity and adaptability in their movements. Flowing from one technique to the next allows practitioners to maintain pressure on opponents and capitalize on openings as they arise.

• **Controlled Contact and Impact**: Sparring partners in Jow-Ga Kung Fu aim to make controlled contact with techniques, delivering strikes and kicks with sufficient force to simulate realistic combat scenarios without causing injury. Practitioners learn to gauge distance, timing, and intensity to strike targets accurately while minimizing the risk of injury to themselves and their opponents.

• **Feints and Setups**: Feints and setups are used to deceive opponents and create opportunities for effective attacks in sparring. Practitioners employ feints to draw out reactions from opponents and exploit openings created by their responses. Setups involve using combinations, footwork, and angles to position oneself for favorable engagements and capitalize on opponents' vulnerabilities.

• **Strategy and Adaptability**: Sparring in Jow-Ga Kung Fu requires practitioners to employ strategic thinking and adaptability to respond effectively to opponents' actions and adjustments. Practitioners analyze opponents' movements, identify patterns and weaknesses, and adjust their tactics accordingly to gain a tactical advantage and control the flow of the match.

- **Respect and Sportsmanship**: Sparring sessions in Jow-Ga Kung Fu emphasize respect, sportsmanship, and mutual learning between practitioners. Participants adhere to ethical guidelines and demonstrate courtesy, humility, and integrity during sparring exchanges, fostering a positive training environment conducive to growth and development.

Overall, sparring in Jow-Ga Kung Fu serves as a valuable training tool for practitioners to refine their techniques, develop martial skills, and test their abilities in a realistic, dynamic setting. Through consistent practice and engagement in sparring, practitioners improve their proficiency, confidence, and understanding of combat principles, enhancing their overall martial arts journey.

Weapons Training, Techniques And Forms With Weapons

In Jow-Ga Kung Fu, weapons training is an integral aspect of martial arts practice, encompassing a variety of traditional Chinese weapons such as staffs, swords, spears, and many others.

Weapons training provide practitioners with additional tools for self-defense, enhance their understanding of martial principles, and add depth to their overall martial arts repertoire. Here's an overview of weapons training, techniques, and forms with weapons in Jow-Ga Kung Fu:

Weapons Training:

- **Staff (Gun)**: The staff is one of the most common weapons used in Jow-Ga Kung Fu. Practitioners learn various techniques for wielding the staff, including striking, blocking, thrusting, and spinning. Staff training emphasizes coordination, timing, and proper grip to effectively wield the weapon for offense and defense.

- **Sword (Jian)**: Sword training in Jow-Ga Kung Fu involves learning traditional Chinese swordsmanship techniques. Practitioners study cutting, thrusting, parrying, and footwork techniques with the sword, focusing on precision, control, and fluidity of movement.

- **Spear (Qiang)**: Spear training emphasizes long-range attacks, thrusts, and thrusting techniques with the spear. Practitioners learn to use the spear's length and leverage to maintain distance from opponents while delivering powerful strikes and thrusts.

- **Broad Sword (Dao)**: Broad sword training focuses on close-range combat techniques with the dao, a single-edged

Chinese saber. Practitioners learn slashing, chopping, and blocking techniques with the broadsword, utilizing its curved blade for effective cutting and defense.

• **Double-edged Sword (Gim)**: Training with the double-edged sword involves mastering techniques for both offensive and defensive purposes. Practitioners learn to wield the sword with precision and speed, executing quick strikes, thrusts, and counters against opponents.

• **Kwan Dao**: The kwan dao is a traditional Chinese polearm with a curved blade resembling a halberd. Training with the kwan dao focuses on powerful sweeping strikes, thrusts, and spins, utilizing the weapon's weight and momentum for maximum impact.

- **Whip Chain (Bian)**: The whip chain is a flexible weapon consisting of metal segments connected by chain links. Practitioners learn to manipulate the whip chain with fluid movements, executing strikes, wraps, and entanglements to control and immobilize opponents.

Techniques and Forms with Weapons:

- **Weapon Techniques**: Techniques with weapons in Jow-Ga Kung Fu include basic strikes, blocks, thrusts, parries, sweeps, and disarms specific to each weapon. Practitioners drill these techniques repetitively to develop proficiency, coordination, and muscle memory with their chosen weapon.

- **Weapon Forms (Tao)**: Weapon forms, also known as "tao" or "kata," are choreographed sequences of movements that simulate combat scenarios with weapons. Each weapon in Jow-Ga Kung Fu typically has its own set of forms, which practitioners learn and practice to refine their technique, footwork, timing, and application of techniques in a structured manner.

- **Two-Person Weapon Drills**: Two-person weapon drills involve practicing techniques, counters, and combinations with a training partner using weapons. These drills enhance practitioners' ability to read and respond to opponents' movements, understand timing and distance, and apply techniques effectively in a dynamic, interactive setting.

- **Weapon Sparring (Tui Shou)**: Weapon sparring, or "tui shou," involves simulated combat with weapons against a resisting opponent. Practitioners engage in controlled, dynamic exchanges using their chosen weapon, applying techniques learned in training while adapting to opponents' movements and tactics.

- **Weapon Disarms and Counters**: Weapon training in Jow-Ga Kung Fu also includes techniques for disarming opponents and countering their attacks. Practitioners learn to neutralize threats posed by armed adversaries using deflections, locks, throws, and other defensive maneuvers specific to each weapon.

Overall, weapons training in Jow-Ga Kung Fu provide practitioners with valuable skills for self-defense, enhance their understanding of martial principles, and enrich their martial arts journey with the study of traditional Chinese weapons and techniques. Through dedicated practice and study, practitioners develop proficiency, versatility, and adaptability in wielding weapons effectively in combat situations.

CHAPTER SEVEN
Practical Application And Strategy With Weapons

In Jow-Ga Kung Fu, practical application and strategy with weapons involve understanding the characteristics of the weapon being used, assessing the situation, and applying appropriate techniques and tactics to achieve desired outcomes in combat scenarios. Here's how practical application and strategy with weapons are approached in Jow-Ga Kung Fu:

• **Understanding Weapon Characteristics**: Practitioners begin by understanding the unique characteristics of the weapon they are using, including its length, weight, balance, and striking surfaces. Each weapon has advantages and limitations that must be considered when formulating strategies for combat. For example, a staff may excel at long-range strikes and thrusts, while a broadsword may be more effective in close-range engagements.

- **Assessing the Situation**: Before engaging in combat with a weapon, practitioners assess the situation to determine factors such as the number and skill level of opponents, available space, terrain, and potential threats. This assessment helps practitioners formulate a strategy tailored to the specific circumstances they are facing, maximizing their chances of success while minimizing risk.

- **Choosing the Right Weapon**: Depending on the situation and personal preference, practitioners may choose different weapons to suit their needs and objectives. For example, a long-range weapon like a spear may be preferred for engaging multiple opponents at a distance, while a shorter weapon like a broadsword may be more suitable for close-quarters combat or confined spaces.

- **Offensive Strategies**: Offensive strategies with weapons in Jow-Ga Kung Fu involve using the weapon to control the distance, set up attacks, and exploit opponents' weaknesses.

Practitioners may employ techniques such as feints, combinations, and angles of attack to create openings and overwhelm opponents with swift, decisive strikes.

- **Defensive Strategies**: Defensive strategies with weapons focus on protecting oneself from incoming attacks while maintaining the ability to counter effectively. Practitioners use blocking, parrying, and evasive footwork to deflect strikes and minimize the impact of opponents' attacks. They also learn to maintain proper distance and positioning to avoid being trapped or overwhelmed by opponents.

- **Adaptability and Versatility:** Effective weapon combat in Jow-Ga Kung Fu requires adaptability and versatility to respond to changing circumstances and opponents' actions. Practitioners learn to adjust their strategies and techniques on the fly, improvising and innovating as needed to gain a tactical advantage and control the flow of the fight.

- **Exploiting Weapon Advantages:** Each weapon in Jow-Ga Kung Fu has its own strengths and advantages, which practitioners seek to exploit during combat. For example, a staff may be used to keep opponents at bay with its reach, while a sword may be used to target specific vulnerable areas with precision and speed. Practitioners learn to leverage these advantages to maximize the effectiveness of their chosen weapon.

- **Maintaining Composure and Focus**: In the heat of combat, practitioners must maintain composure and focus to execute techniques effectively and make sound decisions under pressure. They learn to control their breathing, manage adrenaline, and stay mentally alert and present throughout the engagement.

- **Training Realism and Scenario-based Practice**: To enhance practical application and strategy with weapons, practitioners engage in realistic training drills and scenario-based practice. This involves simulating various combat scenarios, including different opponents, environments, and weapon combinations, to develop adaptive problem-solving skills and muscle memory for effective weapon use in real-world situations.

By incorporating these principles into their training regimen, practitioners of Jow-Ga Kung Fu cultivate strategic thinking and practical application with weapons that exhibit high efficacy, versatility, and adaptability across an extensive spectrum of combat situations.

By engaging in consistent and diligent training, individuals improve their capacity to defend themselves and others in armed combat scenarios with assurance and expertise.

Integration Of Jow-Ga Into Everyday Life

There is more to integrating Jow-Ga Kung Fu into one's daily life than attending classes and honing techniques in the training hall. The process entails incorporating the mindset, values, and principles that are nurtured via martial arts training into diverse facets of one's everyday existence. Incorporate Jow-Ga Kung Fu into the following aspects of your daily life:

• Physical Fitness Consistent physical activity is an essential component of training for Jow-Ga Kung Fu. Daily flexibility activities, cardiovascular exercise, strength training, and stretching should be incorporated into the regimen in order to preserve overall fitness and improve martial arts performance.

• Mindfulness and Meditation: Develop mental concentration, clarity, and tranquility through the practice of mindfulness and meditation techniques. Each day, devote a few moments to sitting attentively, observing your thoughts and emotions without judgment, and concentrating on your breath. In daily life, this practice can aid in tension reduction, concentration improvement, and self-awareness.

- Habits of a Healthy Lifestyle: Adopt healthful lifestyle practices, including adequate rest, nutrition, and hydration, as well as stress management strategies. Ensure that you prioritize your physical and mental health by making decisions that align with your martial arts training and overarching health objectives.

- Adopt the principles of perseverance and discipline that are ingrained in the Jow-Ga Kung Fu training regimen. Develop objectives for yourself in martial arts practice and other spheres of life, and strive conscientiously to accomplish them. Maintain a steadfast dedication to your training regimen by consistently attending sessions and exerting effort to enhance your performance.

• Courtesy and Respect: Ensure that your interactions with others within and beyond the training venue are characterized by courtesy and respect. It is essential to cultivate a positive and supportive training environment by behaving with respect, humility, and kindness towards instructors, training companions, and fellow practitioners.

• Implementation of Conflict Resolution and Self-Control Principles: Employ the self-control and conflict resolution skills acquired through martial arts training in routine circumstances. Demonstrate composure and poise when confronted with difficult situations; employ tact, compassion, and confidence to reconcile disputes and preserve harmonious relationships.

- The Importance of Ongoing Development and Learning: Foster a mindset that prioritizes ongoing development and learning, actively pursuing opportunities to broaden your horizons, expertise, and practical encounters beyond the confines of the classroom. Maintain a receptive attitude towards novel concepts, viewpoints, and obstacles, approaching the process of personal and martial arts growth with inquisitiveness and eagerness.

- Cultivate self-awareness regarding one's environment and potential hazards in routine activities, employing self-defense principles and tactics to ensure one's own safety and, if required, safeguard the well-being of others. Remain vigilant, exercise confidence in your intuition, and be ready to respond in order to safeguard your welfare and security.

- Community Engagement: Contribute to the growth and development of the martial arts community through active participation. Engage in seminars, workshops, and events; assist fellow practitioners on their martial arts journeys; and impart your expertise and experiences to others.

By incorporating the principles and practices of Jow-Ga Kung Fu into one's daily routine, it is possible to develop and maintain physical fitness, mental fortitude, ethical principles, and practical abilities that contribute to an enhanced quality of life and improved efficacy across multiple domains.

Summary

Jow-Ga Kung Fu presents a comprehensive methodology for martial arts instruction, which includes not only technical mastery, but also mental fortitude, ethical principles, and physical fitness. By means of consistent effort and unwavering devotion, individuals who engage in Jow-Ga Kung Fu cultivate not only physical prowess and combat expertise, but also cognitive concentration, emotional fortitude, and moral rectitude.

The fundamental tenets of Jow-Ga Kung Fu encompass effective techniques, correct body positioning, internal energy cultivation, and pragmatic implementation in combat situations; collectively, they offer an all-encompassing structure for individual growth and self-protection. Through the incorporation of these principles into their day-to-day existence, individuals foster physical fitness, emotional equilibrium, moral integrity, and mental lucidity, thereby augmenting their holistic welfare and making constructive contributions to their respective communities.

In all settings, including training rooms, workplaces, and casual conversations, individuals who practice Jow-Ga Kung Fu exemplify the virtues of perseverance, humility, respect, and discipline. They exhibit bravery, flexibility, and resolve when confronted with obstacles, embracing the process of ongoing development and progress both within and beyond the athletic arena.

Jow-Ga Kung Fu transcends its status as a mere martial art and transcends into a lifestyle—one that promotes holistic well-being, personal empowerment, and self-discovery. By engaging in the supplication of Jow-Ga Kung Fu, individuals endeavor to develop not only their martial prowess but also their character, fostering equilibrium, empathy, and fortitude in order to actualize their full potential and effectuate a constructive influence on the global community.

THE END

Made in the USA
Monee, IL
05 April 2024

56435046R00056